21st Century Emperor

Emperor

DAVID BLACK

1

Contents

About This Book

We were told that the only path to success and happiness is university education followed by years committed to a stable career. We were educated to become productive employees, but never to own the fruits of our life's labour. Almost all of us (the author included), fell into this trap.

The truth though, is that we spend our best years, working for someone else. Soldiers building other men's empires.

This book aims to show you a second path.

Written for people who want more from their life, providing lessons to individuals who want to work for themselves and be master of their own destiny. It teaches how you can ruthlessly apply strategy on your daily activities, focusing energy on areas of high leverage that take you closer to your personal objectives.

It is not lack of options in the world, but their abundance that weighs us down. We are paralysed by it. Opportunity is everywhere. There's almost so much choice we can't see it for what it is. Your success will come from focusing energy on one of those opportunities, for long enough to be able to profit from a better one, that you're now in a position to take advantage of. When you have chosen the right opportunity, you simply have to devise and execute a clear plan that concentrates your forces on the points of leverage that get you closer to what you want.

The book encourages you to build your own empire, however small, to decouple how you earn your money and spend your time. An empire that not only works for you, but also sets you free.

Fused with these lessons is a story of how the author quit his job in London, built a mini empire and became a digital nomad with true financial and location independence. As a cautionary note though, this book rejects the concept of the "overnight success". Instead the information is a guide for building a stable empire that gives you freedom and real options in your own life.

The focus is on location independent business models that can be executed online and the growing numbers of digital nomads who are using their empire's to lead extraordinary lives.

David Black,

Chiang Mai, Thailand 2016

Operation Freedom

The pursuit of financial freedom has always been a worthwhile endeavour. Today though, in a world of economic uncertainty and the near collapse of social security, it is the only sensible course of action. Individuals can no longer rely on employers or governments to look after their long term financial interests. Expecting other people to be able to provide for you in your waning years is the riskiest bet you have ever taken.

It's also the most important one to get right.

The Industrial Revolution ended almost a century ago, yet the social construction that made it so successful at the time, now serves to cap our potential today. We are educated to succeed as productive employees, but never to become financially independent ourselves.

We are encouraged instead to take out debt, in the form of higher education loans, home mortgages and cheap credit, all forcing us to work harder, for longer, while retaining ever less of the rewards of our labour, health and time. The answer of course, is investing. Any employee who starts prudently saving their income from a young age, is very likely to have a pleasant retirement, as long as they live long enough to enjoy it. This book though, is about a different kind of investing. It's going to teach you how to invest in yourself. To learn how to build a network of assets that are going to work tirelessly for you, every day and night.

These assets will be your empire.

A small empire to be sure, but with digital technology, time, a clear strategy and focused effort, you can become the master of your own destiny.

You will not have to work for, or rely on any other individual again for your income and no one will dictate to you how and where you are to spend your days. It is now possible to learn any skill and sell almost any product or service online by yourself, therefore you no longer need an employer to bring value to the market place. With the right tools, skills and strategies you can build your own mini empire. An empire designed to decouple how you spend your time and how you earn your money. This point alone is enough to ensure the security of your financial future, while enabling the ultimate freedom of true location independence.

With that in mind though, I want to make a point perfectly clear. This book is not about "getting rich quick" and I certainly do not believe in the concept of the "overnight success".

I am not rich, so could not with good conscience, publish advice on that subject. Instead this book is the story of how I built my empire. The lessons drawn are from my failures and the experiences have been recorded to guide you, as you navigate the murky waters of enterprise. While the journey is a long and risky one, it's the only true route to freedom and power. In the context of this book, freedom and power are two sides of the same coin.

Power is to be re-conceptualized, not as control over other people, but rather; control over your own actions. In this sense, you have power to the extent that other people do not have power over you. The more areas of your life that you have the freedom to choose, the more powerful you have become. Under this definition, having a boss diminishes your power. Self-employment however, does not necessitate it either.

Many people run successful businesses, but are also trapped by them. Fixing their schedules, location and attention. These businesses can make you rich, but they don't all set you free. The focus then. in our pursuit of freedom, will be on business models that can be executed online, from anywhere in the world you choose.

The examples are models that have been tried by either myself, or the growing numbers of location independent entrepreneurs (digital nomads) who are using their empires to bring them freedom, financial independence and personal power.

After quitting my job in London in 2010 with no resources, idea or plan, I eventually built a series of digital assets that gave me the freedom to move to Asia and never have to work for another person again.

Those assets are my Empire and I want to use this book to show you exactly how to build one too. The kind of empire you create will be up to you, but this book will help you to conceive and engineer it specifically to allow you to do the things you want to do and live the kind of life that you want to lead. For me that means travelling the world while working a few hours a day on the projects that I'm interested in (such as this book). For you it could be something different, perhaps spending more time with your family, or sailing the globe. Whatever it is you want from life, you can make it happen by building your own empire.

The Road to Freedom

It all started 6 years ago. Fresh out of university, I was on my way to London to start my new life as a professional within the insurance industry. At the time I remember thinking I was on the road to success. I had studied hard, passed my exams and been accepted onto a graduate management program with a respectable company. In a few years I thought, I would have real options, money and freedom. Any illusions I had though, driving down to London to start my new life, were quickly exposed to be just that, illusions. No one was getting rich in that place and certainly no one was securing any meaningful levels of options or freedom.

The more time and energy they put into their work, deeper into the rabbit hole they went. The senior management did reasonably well for themselves I'm sure, but any additional income they had gained was directly proportionate to the extra time and responsibility that was required of them.

Money and freedom it seemed were two mutually exclusive concepts. To have one, you needed to sacrifice the other.

My frustration with the new life I found myself in, essentially being an employee of a large corporation, started to build rapidly. Not only was the prospect of getting trapped on the greasy pole of promotion particularly unappealing, but the fact that at the end of the day I didn't own the product of my labour was becoming more and more unacceptable. My time and energy were being traded for money, but all of the long term benefits were being retained by someone else.

I felt like a soldier working for an empire. Orders came down the line and I was expected to execute them without question, regardless of whether it was a cause I believed worth fighting for or not. What had I let myself get into?

Every aspect of the organisation's policies and cultures seemed designed to foster a dependency relationship with "the empire". From the politics around pay grades to the company share scheme, the corporate objective was clear. Keep working for us.

I needed to find a way out. I didn't want to be a pawn on someone else's chess board, however large and comfortable. I wanted to start my own operation and build wealth for myself. If I could find people to do it for me, all the better. The problem of course was that I had no idea how to start one. I had qualifications, but no skills. I had references, but no experience. The sad fact is, that despite all of the years spent in high school, college and university, my real education only began the day I decided to learn how to support myself in the business world.

I had always been industrious and entrepreneurial as a child, cleaning cars in the local neighbourhood at around age 12 then selling sunglasses and jeans at high school. But the idea of actually "starting a business" had never really been a clear goal.

The reason for this I believe is how we have been raised and educated. In many upwardly mobile households, business is something of a dubious and dirty word. Parents want their children to graduate from medical or law schools, not opening shops, renting trucks and hustling for orders. Enterprise isn't on the school curriculum and there's no prospectus for colleges teaching students how to actually start, grow and sell companies. Instead, "business degrees" and "MBA's" are really just courses designed to train future managers.

The path we are encouraged to take is one of increasing amounts of specialisation into narrow fields as we pass through school and university.

This we are told, is our route to success.

The truth though is that it just saddles us with debt and in most cases provides no real benefits in term of career advantage, simply due to the fact that there are so many more graduates now, fighting for the same number of jobs.

With my mind racing around these ideas and the possibilities of starting different types of enterprises, motivation for the day job was at an all-time low, it simply had to go. I was so preoccupied, thinking about and building the enterprise that I wasn't really that effective in the office any more.

Focus was needed, and perhaps earlier than I should have, I handed in my resignation.

Looking back, the problem wasn't really splitting my time with work and the new project. It would have been both a sensible and sustainable solution while the business was being incubated. The real issue was that at that time I had no real skills, nothing to offer the market place and a complete lack of clarity in the direction I needed to take. I simply wasn't clear with myself about what I wanted, so all of the early projects I tried inevitably floundered.

I was obsessed with finding the "big idea", which led me to create ridiculous products such as a new genital wart treatment and an online magazine documenting changes in UK climate compliance. All of which (quite rightly) didn't make a penny.

The key of course was not to find a 'brilliant business idea', but instead to pick a good business model and do it better than the competition. New ideas are untested, slow to reach the market and very expensive to protect. Existing business models on the other hand can be analysed and compared against a framework of requirements that you determine for yourself. These requirements could be anything from the amount of money you have to spend, which rules out any options with higher entry costs than you can afford, to the general attractiveness of the business model itself with respect to your skills, passions or temperament.

It took me a long time before I put pen to paper and detailed exactly what I needed from the enterprise. My framework ruled out 99.9% of the options available, because I had absolutely nothing to invest and the only piece of equipment I owned was a laptop.

As it turns out though, that still left me with a huge amount of choice in the business models that were available.

It is vitally important to ask yourself what it is that you want the business to do for you. Simply "making money" is not a clear enough objective. For a long time, I thought that what I wanted was just to be rich and if I was being perfectly honest, I didn't really care how I got there. There are a number of issues with this though, all of which held me back. To start with, being rich isn't a "goal" as much as it is a state of affairs. Saying to myself that I wanted to be rich is similar to the statement, "I want to live until I'm 80". It very well may happen, but it offers nothing in the way of clarity of how I got there or what my standard of living was going to be during the process.

We need focus and concentration of effort to reach meaningful objectives and without this, there's almost no hope of getting there.

It was only when I started to define for myself what it was that "being rich" enabled, that I started to make progress. I didn't necessarily want large amounts of cash, but just enough so that I could do all of the things I wanted to do while never having to worry about money. I've never been interested in fast cars, but I was interested in travel. I wanted to work, but I prefer to work alone and certainly didn't want to have to go into an office every day. I didn't want to have a boss, but at the same time, the prospect of babysitting staff was almost as unappealing. In short I needed to refine my objectives.

What I really wanted was freedom.

Freedom to go anywhere and do anything, without having to ask permission or suffer the financial consequences of throwing in the towel on a particular project, client or employer.

The world is a big place and spending my day's window gazing and clock watching from the office had become increasingly hard to bear. Real freedom like this was something that I had previously believed was only available to the rich and perhaps why it took me so long to get started, eventually realising that this wasn't necessarily the case.

You don't need a large pot of cash to be free, you simply need a small pot that is being passively refilled as quickly as you are draining it. That shift in thinking made everything else possible.

I didn't need to make a million bucks, I just needed to make a thousand or two every month. I didn't need to run a large company, I just needed to own a profitable one. I didn't need to be rich, I just needed to be free.

Empire Builder

The idea that my business was an empire started as a joke. One of my best friends would ask almost every day, "how's the empire today David?". The joke of course was that at the time my enterprise was so small, it was doubtful that it deserved the title of "business", let alone anything so grandiose as "empire". But the more I thought about it, reflecting on the experiences I had working for other people and other corporations, I realised that actually he wasn't too far from the mark. My enterprise was an empire, just an extremely small one. I was the leader of the operation and its purpose was to secure financial independence and ultimately, my freedom.

I was the emperor and the empire pushed forward my agenda. It was the vehicle with which I could force my will upon reality, taking me closer to the lifestyle I wanted. Using the analogy cast a spirit of adventure over my endeavours, as I forged ahead into the unchartered territories of enterprise.

Whatever kind of business you pick, make no mistake about it, it's a kind of war. Whether you're a web developer or Yoga teacher, you have a clear theatre of operations. There's a certain amount of clients in the market and other entrepreneurs are fighting to secure as bigger share of the spoils as they can get. There's always someone with more cash to throw into their marketing and there are even more people willing to offer the same solutions for less than you could possibly afford to provide them.

It's your job to outwit them all, by using your resources more strategically, making it possible for you to offer more value to the marketplace than your competitors.

That's the key you know, value. For those of you who think, like I used to, in terms of "how much can I make?", you can learn a lesson here. It is only when you start operating from the paradigm of "how much value can I provide?" that things will start to happen for you. The options in your life are directly related to the amount of value that you bring to the marketplace. For employees, calculating the amount of value you add is easy to spot. It is reflected exactly in the wage you have agreed to and the return on investment from your assets. No more, no less.

Your lifestyle will reflect to a large degree whatever figure that is. For an entrepreneur it's slightly more complex as your business retains value in addition to the money you earn. You can for example, sell the business. The principle is essentially the same though, the more value your business can bring to the marketplace, the better your lifestyle options will be. Value, and how to add more of it should be the modus operandi of your empire.

Many of my closest friends are business owners. The reason for this is that it's something I'm passionate about. I've always been envious of football fans, simply for the fact that when two of them meet for the first time, they have a lot of common ground to talk about and it's extremely easy for them to build rapport.

The same is true for me when I meet entrepreneurs and often we become fast friends. Many of these friends are extremely successful, they have large numbers of staff, fast cars and expensive houses. What most of them lack however is freedom. In many ways they have little more freedom than the employees that work for them. They can take a plane to Paris for lunch, but on Monday morning they need to be back to open up. These types of bricks and mortar businesses are empires in their own right and they make lots of money. But they are not the subject of this book.

This book is about using business to secure freedom. The business models I want to map out then, all share one particular characteristic. They operate independently of any one fixed location.

I'm typing these words from a city called Chiang Mai in Northern Thailand. Apart from it being an amazing city with some of the lowest living costs in the world, one of the other reason I'm here is that it's currently the world's largest hub for digital nomads. There are at last count, (from the Chiang Mai Digital Nomad Facebook page membership figures) 10,000 western entrepreneurs living in this one small city. All of them using their digital empires to support their extraordinary lives.

It is these business models that I want to focus on, because it is these businesses that are providing their owners with genuine freedom, financial security and creative fulfilment. There are 3 categories of these business models and in many cases (mine included) location independent entrepreneurs have formed their empires out of a combination of assets spread between the different categories:

1. **Service Empires**

2. **Product Empires**

3. **Information Empires**

Which model you choose will be determined largely by the skills and resources you have at your disposal today, or could reasonably hope to secure in the short term future. Each category will have very different ramifications on your time, risk exposure and work life balance so it's a decision not to be taken lightly. Before you decide on the character of your empire though, you need an accurate map of the battlefield, a fixed destination and a plan to get you there on the most efficient route.

Imperial Strategy

Strategy is one of the most misused concepts in business literature, often interchanged randomly with notions of tactics, goals and plans. **Strategy** however, is simply the execution of a series of **tactics**, which help you reach a desired **objective**, nothing more nor less. In this sense it is appears to be a quite straightforward concept, but rarely is it exercised rigorously by individuals and organisations, who fail to outline and act upon all three of the elements in the strategic equation.

In the early years of my entrepreneurial adventure, the progress of growth was not linear. If you plotted it on a graph somehow, it would look like shark teeth, racing up for 6 months and then crashing. The reason for that was because I was making as many bad decisions as good ones. There was no clear and attainable objective, so all of my actions were reactive.

This constantly left me wide open for whatever opportunity or risk came along without being able to cross check ideas against a pre-existing, well thought out plan. Before we can start to even think about devising a strategy for your scheme, you need an unequivocal objective. My first objective was to get rich, which isn't a real objective at all, because it's not a definable goal.

In any case, it still hasn't happened and just staying in the game and avoiding the return to paid employment was the priority at many points over the last few years. It took a long time and a lot of reading to finally know what strategy really meant and how to implement it effectively in my life and business. I use the word 'know' in the sense that the knowledge changed how I acted in a positive way, not just my understanding of the concept in the purely academic (and superficial) sense.

Towards the end of 2015, when my landlord tried to force me to sign another rental agreement for 12 months, I made the decision to move to Thailand. It was something that I had been talking about for years, but never came close to taking action. With big decisions like that, you can dream and plan all you like, but unless you make it an objective of absolute priority, it will be postponed indefinitely. Another year though, spent half-heartedly serving clients with marketing consultancy online, from a bedroom in Sheffield would have driven me insane. I was already unhappy, sedated by boredom and frequently anxious of cruising through daily activities semi-consciously, exercising but a fraction of my potential. Time cared little for my shortcomings of course and rolled by at a mockingly accelerated pace. Days passing without observable growth was as much a driver for change as the economic benefits leaving the grossly overpriced United Kingdom. Dropping myself in Asia with nothing more than a bag and my wits was the perfect solution for both.

That is not to say though that Thailand would have been the only cure. The anxiety endured during a life wasted in activity far below your potential and the frustration felt with access to limited resources are both caused by the acceptance of being slowly tethered to mediocrity. Any objective which pushed me to the edge of my comfort zone, exposed me to a healthy dose of risk and provided the opportunity for new projects, would have been sufficient to defibrillate me out of my indolence.

The flight was booked 6 weeks ahead and for the first time since applying for a job in London, I had an absolutely clear and actionable objective:

Objective: In a month and half, I am going to get on that flight and be in a financial position to stay in Thailand indefinitely.

Only with a clear objective, is it time to begin developing your strategy and the tactics that execute it. We proceed then to the first order of business - Developing a strategy.

To be able to live comfortably in Asia I needed to have enough cash. My consulting practice and some of the information assets I had acquired were doing well enough for me to live in England, so in theory at least I could afford to live in the much cheaper city of Chiang Mai. Living in the overpriced United Kingdom didn't leave me with that much spare capital, which was not a problem in the low risk environment of my home town, but for being in Asia alone, I needed more.

I wanted to change how I made my money too, not just delivering services, but earning money passively, finally breaking those last chains linking money and time. I devised two strategies, one short term (6 weeks), and another medium term (9 Months). The short term strategy was to raise as much cash as possible before I left and the tactics within that strategy are obvious to all. Essentially; sell everything I don't need and work really, really hard. The longer term strategy required much more thought though. How can I make money, live in Thailand and not have to talk to, or directly work for clients? The solution was a twofold approach. First, use the advantage of Thailand's lower cost of living to free up resources and re-invest them into developing product and information assets, which contributed to building an empire that did meet my lifestyle requirements.

Then secondly, I would harness the unique resources and opportunities in Chiang Mai. Not only is the cost of living and goods significantly cheaper here and the level of craftsmanship so high, but there is also access to products that simply aren't available in the UK or US, yet do have a rightful place on a given digital marketplace. 'These products are bought by thousands, if not millions of tourists each year' I thought, 'so why not on Amazon too?'. Other benefits of buying locally include the ease of which you can resolve supplier problems, which have occurred numerously and will invariably continue to do so. There have been many occasions, such as when returning stock or ordering new custom variations that my thankfulness has validated the benefit of not having to liaise with Chinese companies. These were both coherent principles that would help me to make good decisions, driving me in a straight line towards my goal of true financial and location independence. Your strategy should be as simple as this too, it doesn't need to be long and convoluted like the intricate mind maps I used to draw in sketch pads at length. Instead they look like this:

Strategic Directive #1: Run the consulting business at full steam ahead, generating as much revenue as possible. Use all of the money saved by living in Chiang Mai to invest in the product and information empire.

Strategic Directive #2: Build a series of product and information assets that utilise resources unique to Chiang Mai, which have a large disparity in value between Thailand and the western marketplaces online.

With this level of clarity, I can start to outline my tactics and get started on taking meaningful, high impact action. For the first directive it was simple.

Just carry on doing what you have been doing for years and don't go crazy with spending money in the first few months. The second directive required me go out and find the opportunities that fitted my new requirements of earning money as efficiently as possible (preferably passively) without the need to serve clients directly. For the product empire I wanted to find a range of locally made items that could be featured together in a curated shop. I needed quick resupply times, low minimum wholesale order volumes and most of all a big gap between the price in town and similar items on websites like Amazon and Etsy.

Only a fraction of a percent of the items out there were appropriate, but with enough time and some wasted money on misguided purchases, they would be found. For I would simply keep looking. Making the empire's next few moves into information assets was harder.

Finding a way to draw value from the resources in Chiang Mai kept me thinking for some time. Until I realised that the experience of being here and the story of how it happened, was a resource in and of itself. A particularly unique and potentially valuable resource that only I could extract. This book and the Digital Nomad X YouTube channel were born that day.

What constitutes an objective, strategy or tactic depends on whereabouts in the chain you are looking. The plan above was my high level strategy. The strategy and tactics are designed to focus energy on particular points of leverage such as the consulting business, visiting local manufacturers and suppliers or making more YouTube episodes for example. However, for many of these high level tactics, like maintaining the consulting business, they have their own set of objectives, strategies and tactics.

The tactics for the consulting business include SEO, upselling, email marketing and CRM improvements, among many others. Similarly, if you have a boss, some of their tactics will be all of your objectives. Your strategy will of course be different to mine because you will have a different vision about what you want from your life. For those of you seeking real freedom though, rather than the extreme poles of wage slavery or obscene riches, your strategy should include self-employment as an absolute minimum. Ideally the strategy will seek to secure you, over time, a growing portfolio of assets. These will vary from capital investments like real estate and financial instruments, to retail infrastructure that allows you to access revenue digitally. With low capital though, you may need to undertake services for a while, until you have finished building a route over the barriers to entry into products and information operations.

Without any capital, you have almost zero access to revenue from financial investments. Before you can start buying these (or any) assets, you need to own an empire that can afford them. Living and profiting off the dividends of your stocks, shares and bonds is the ultimate form of financial freedom. For most of us of course, myself included, we have to start in the mud, piecing together a service or retail empire with bare hands and crude tools until we can afford the entry fee into more desirable tournaments.

Whichever assets you are seeking to acquire; you should do so alone. My theory on this, is that people get into partnerships because they lack either resources, skills or confidence. Often a combination of all three. Partnerships are almost always forged from positions of weakness. While this may seem like a particularly blunt and insensitive proposition, there is a logic to it that's hard to counter.

If we have the resources, skills and confidence to execute a project on our own, why would we ever sign up to give away half of the loot? Not only this but working co-dependently is almost by definition, anathema to freedom. Having said that though, I have absolutely no issue with partnering with people on side projects. You can learn a lot and achieve things you couldn't on your own. But it is just a side project, not your main business, on which the fate of everything depends. If the side project succeeds without detriment to your other enterprises, then it is a success. If it doesn't succeed, the loss is limited and knowledge is gained. You can just carry on building your main empire and put the whole experience down as one more valuable lesson.

When you spend time working on your objectives, strategies and tactics, the hardest part is often choosing which of the in-numeral choices available to focus energy on.

It is not lack of options, but their abundance which weighs us down. We are paralysed by it. Opportunity is everywhere. There's almost so much choice we can't see it for what it is. Your success will come from focusing energy on one of those opportunities, for long enough to be able to profit from a better one, that you're now in a position to take advantage of. When you have chosen the right opportunity, you simply have to devise and execute a clear plan that concentrates your forces on the points of leverage that get you closer to what you want. Regularly ask yourself, 'am I focusing my energy on activities that matter?'. You don't need to just do one thing, but for all of the important things you are doing, consistently focus on activities that have the most impact.

Applying the lens of your strategy will force you to make better decisions.

In the past I could have been accused of jumping on any opportunity that floated by. Being burned repeatedly though fosters caution and for many years after, I avoided them completely. In fact, opportunities presented themselves even more frequently when I moved to Chiang Mai, but armed with strategy, I had reference points to guide my decisions. Most of the shiny prospects that appeared while in Asia didn't fit into the framework I had outlined, so were passed on, politely. When a friend and fellow ex pat living in Chiang Mai wanted to sell his Etsy store however, it was immediately obvious that this asset slotted perfectly into the second strategic directive. It was a complete business, already generating revenue and had secured some good reviews. The artwork and branding were considerably better than my own Etsy start-up and the additional extras he included with the product packaging were a really nice touch. All of this could be (and was) quickly incorporated into my fledgling product empire. Not only this, but the product range and supplier relations he had built were with local Chiang Mai manufactures. I could ship them in small envelopes meaning the postal cost were extremely low and the profit margins were over 1000%. It ticked all of the boxes so I moved decisively to acquire it before any other grubby hands started presenting their own offers of interest.

For almost all types of business one of the biggest impact areas is marketing. The best tactics build assets as you execute them, not just display text ads to random audiences on forums for 30 days. For instance, regular social media activity has the secondary benefit of increasing long term visibility of your website on Google.

Developing a set of explainer videos for your product or service will increase conversions, but can also be re-used in other areas of your marketing to raise awareness or build the brand. Your business will grow to the extent you can develop and improve these assets, which can be defined as any platform, digital or otherwise, that generates leads and revenue. The value of the asset is measured in how efficiently (with respect to time and labour) it generates or contributes to sustainable profits.

The tactics employed in your arsenal will ultimately depend on the directives within your strategy. Whether you are choosing to focus energy on SEO and social media or advertisements and content marketing you should think about them as pieces of artillery and the individual actions taken, as the ammunition.

The more your big guns are calibrated, the better chance you have for your actions landing on target, pushing forward your agenda with devastating precision. For example, lets imagine (in the hypothetical presence of perfect information) we discover there are 87 steps that need to be taken to 100% optimise a particular website for maximum visibility on search engines. An individual who performs each task, one after the other, would be executing his SEO marketing tactic perfectly. Each round of labour smashing through the barriers between the present reality and what he wants it to be - Owning a lucrative asset at the very top of Google search listings for a popular keyword. Your empire is small, so you only need a few extremely well maintained guns with plenty of ammunition. If you are new to marketing it will take time to learn how to operate the tactics you have chosen. My first attempts at off page SEO were laughable. Copying and pasting terrible sales messages into forum posts and wondering why I kept getting banned and people weren't buying.

Just as we need objectives, strategies and tactics for our life's work, the empire, we need them on a micro basis for 'marketing strategy' too. Your tactics will be actions like Pay Per Click (PPC) marketing, SEO, following up leads and email marketing. Which tactics you select and how you allocate resources will be the strategy. Not all of the tactics are suitable for the entrepreneur who is engineering personal freedom though. Call centres do work, but they are extremely human resource intensive. TV advertisements have a huge reach, but they lack precision and cost small fortunes to deploy. Email marketing can be a powerful driver of sales, but you need a large list of people who are interested in what you say.

Your marketing strategy needs to implement a set of carefully selected tactics, that help you to reach your marketing objectives. The first job will be to discover the best target to focus resources (time, money and physical labour) on.

Ultimately you need to place yourself in space where your customers are already in, or close to, the psychological mind-set of buying a particular product or service. People browsing #vintageclothes on Pinterest and Instagram could be encouraged to buy related items on your Etsy store. Similarly, a director browsing LinkedIn for potential new recruits, may be interested in talking to a company about improving their payroll system. It's vital for you to identify in your strategy which tactics have the most leverage for your business and then concentrate your forces accordingly. The problem is not a lack of options; quite the reverse.

The challenge is knowing where you should go all in.

This is the essence of Imperial strategy - Identify an absolutely clear objective, then devise a strategy that focuses energy on the highest areas of leverage that help you to reach it. Where possible, implement tactics that acquire assets as they are executed, allowing you to recycle work and recapture expended effort.

Service Empires

In general, services are the easiest types of business to start, but by far the hardest to scale. My first relative success in business was with a service based operation. A few of my friends who had started their companies while I was at university, were savvy entrepreneurs, but they were also for all intents and purposes computer illiterate. They needed help with their Internet marketing and I needed money.

The only thing missing was the actual skills required to help them. A trivial matter though, I thought. They needed websites, so I just needed to learn how to build them. Many hours later spent mainly on YouTube, I was finally in a position to start offering real value to my first customers. The fact that these customers were my friends made no real difference. If anything it was essential as they understood and accepted that I was learning as I went along. To this day, they remind me that they, or perhaps I, was the Guinea pig.

More work followed from this. Once their websites were built they needed help to market them. Smelling opportunity, I started learning about Internet marketing, SEO and Google AdWords. Skills which not only found me more eager customers, but also became invaluable in promoting my other business ventures in the years to come.

By the end of the first year I was well on the way to building a little profitable empire. Working hard, quickly rectifying mistakes and trying my best to offer as much value as possible for my clients, demand for my services was starting to increase. In fact, it had grown to such an extent that I needed some help.

It's here that problems started to arise. When you start a service business, in most cases it's just you fulfilling the given service.

Whether you are an electrician, accountant or Piano instructor, as long as you are competent and have the right tools of the trade, you will probably succeed. You simply need the technical ability and a relatively small degree of interpersonal skills (depending on your niche). It is only when you start to grow and scale the business that complications start to creep in. Services are generally fulfilled by people so if you want to provide more services than you can comfortably perform yourself, you need more people.

People though are curious things. Expensive to hire and difficult to manage. I couldn't really afford permanent staff in the office and all of the extra baggage that they entailed. The solution for me was to outsource. I needed to find skilled people overseas who had technical ability while also charging low enough rates for me to maintain profits.

To do this I teamed up with another English marketing agency based in Wimbledon. Together we hired a pair of developers to work in their office in India, which was previously dedicated to purely SEO services. Not knowing how much I should pay for their services, I agreed to terms which were on reflection significantly inflated. I have since learned too that much of the time I bought, was being spent on other unrelated projects. Despite this though my business still turned a healthy profit and relations with the other agency grew closer. So close in fact that when the other agency started talking to venture capitalists about securing expansion finance, I was as invited to the table. I was, it turns out, their biggest client. A point of fact that had I realised at the time, would have made me very wary about getting further involved. I was a crucial foundation of their business and they did not want me to know it.

The venture capitalist was a man named Bill. A millionaire who had from the stories he told, made his fortune buying up German assets during the fall of the Berlin wall and sold them a short while after for huge profits. A smart man by all accounts but also a dishonest one. We spent months organising the details of our new business. I would head up the sales team in Sheffield, while management was to be done in London and operations in India. Agreements were made in principle and I started looking for staff. The problem was that these agreements were only in "principle". I will never forget the statement Bill made at one of our early board meetings, "contracts are great, but trust is better". Noble words indeed. The next few months showed me how naive I really was for putting stock in anything as cheap as words. I'd already started the hiring process by the time Bill told us he was no longer interested in providing the capital for our new agency. I had contracts with these new employees, but none with the man himself. The result was an untenable position. My business had warped from a small, but profitable enterprise into an overstaffed, undercapitalised disaster.

My first mistake was listening to Bill's bullshit. The second was trying to make it work anyhow. The moment he pulled out I should have had a difficult discussion with the staff and let them go as painlessly as possible. They hadn't finished their training, so trying to bring them up to speed, while maintaining the output of work was a virtually impossible task.

My physical and mental health broke down very quickly as I worked day and night trying to mobilise my new found resources while keeping clients and creditors happy. The cash flow situation just wouldn't allow it.

There was more than enough work to support myself, but not the host of new employees who at that time added absolutely no value to the business. I had let the situation play out for too long and when it finally came to letting them go, it wasn't a strategic withdrawal, but rather an abandonment. There was no money to pay them, so they would need to be compensated later.

This was the first, of many business failures and my young empire, very loudly, collapsed in on itself.

I had tried to do the right thing by attempting to make it work, but ultimately I prolonged the misery and probably made a few enemies along the way. It was my first big setback and for many months I slid into a kind of depression.

When things had looked so promising under the light of the venture capital deal, I had moved into a new house and bought a new car. All of which, combined with the repayments I needed to make to the workforce were crippling me financially. Many of the people I had hired were part of my extended social group and the fiasco was extremely public. The stress, coupled with the guilt, were at the time too much for me handle while trying to operate (or in this case, save) a business. I receded like a hermit into the house that I couldn't afford and the months passed me by.

There are many lessons to be taken from this fiasco. One of the most important was my complete neglect of risks that I was exposing my enterprise to. At no point during those mad months, did I stop and see how wide-open I had become.

In so many different ways, the decisions of other people could, and did have an impact on my life, financial security and health. Why did I ever agree to jumping in the boat in the first place? Because I didn't have a clear objective and a real plan to get there. Without directions it's very easy to be distracted by bright lights on the horizon, perhaps even, inevitable.

When I'd pretty much given up on my first venture a friend who had been running a successful dog walking company offered me a job. He was expanding his business and building a huge dog crèche. He had leased a warehouse and needed help converting the premises. I had no experience with that kind of work, and if I'm honest was reluctant to do manual labour, but my options were running out. I was behind on the rent and desperately needed some money.

As it turns out, I really enjoyed the time spent converting the premises. Most of the technical work was done by another friend who was a joiner by trade, but I learned a lot. The biggest lesson I took was a reminder of why I started down this road in the first place. Here I was, literally building someone else's empire. In any case the break did me good. Physical labour is tiring, but it is far from mentally taxing, leaving plenty of time for quiet reflection. After a few months, my energy and motivation had returned and I was ready to start again.

I sold the car, moved out of the expensive house and started living with some friends. It was easy to rebuild the business really, simply because it was a service enterprise. It was back to basics and all I needed to do was offer my technical expertise to the marketplace again.

Clients started to roll in once more. One in particular started to work closely with me. A local T shirt printing company. They had all of the machines, qualified staff and a brilliant finished product. The problem was that they just didn't know how to run a business or market their services. I helped them as much as I could, but they had a divided leadership and it was clear to me that the company was in trouble. I knew that I could do a better job, and smelling another opportunity, made the company an offer. I will create a new T shirt printing company, market it online and send all of the work to them. Essentially taking a cut of the revenue generated and hopefully engendering the skills and systems used to drive sales and manage data more effectively. They agreed to my proposal and within a few months, implementing everything I had learned about Internet marketing, my new enterprise was online and orders started coming through in droves. Success.

Greed changed that though. On the one hand the company I was dealing with were pushing me on prices, squeezing my margins and diminishing my motivation for working with them. On the other hand, I was probably over inflating the amount of value I was bringing to the table. I mean, 'how hard can actually printing the T shirts really be?'. Quite hard, as it turned out. A less ambitious man would have maintained the status quo and been happy with the relatively large amounts of passive income. A smarter man would have looked for other suppliers, haggled prices and made a better deal. I on the other hand elected to start printing the shirts myself, from home.

This was obviously a huge mistake and admittedly, foolhardy & stupid.

Not only did it massively detract my focus from my main business, the marketing agency, but more than that, led me into a battle that I was wholly unprepared and unequipped for. I had no idea how to print a t-shirt, nor how complex and technical the process was. Some of the machinery I bought and some of it I made myself. Miraculously I managed to fulfil quite a few of the early orders. As those orders started to increase though and customers purchased more complex, multi-colour work, I started to head into deeper waters. A big order came through for a big local rock band who were due to perform at the popular 'Tramlines' festival in Sheffield. I bought thousands of blank t-shirts and began to print. It became quite clear though almost immediately that my machinery wasn't up to scratch for this particular job and I ruined t-shirt after t-shirt. The gig was the next day and I hadn't managed to print a single piece properly. Some other machinery broke and one job after the next went wrong, I was in real trouble once again.

Apologetic emails and phone calls followed, but quite rightly these people just wanted their t-shirts delivering or their money returning. Their events had been "ruined" and it was my fault. The problem was that all my money had been spent on buying the materials for the work. My credit was still reeling from the last venture and I found myself in a very deep hole indeed.

A week later I had policemen sitting in my front room asking me to explain myself. Explain I did, but when it came to the officers asking if they could search my house, I thought that it was a step too far and declined. The next moment I was being arrested for fraud and the search proceeded anyway. There was nothing to find in my house of course, except printing equipment, ruined t-shirts and ink everywhere.

All of which should have proved that my intentions were honest, but nevertheless I spent a few hours in a police cell block with time to reflect on my second failed empire.

Once again, many lessons can be drawn from the calamity, For the second time I completely failed to manage the risk. It was only when I had all of my capital tied up in one job and each t-shirt in the job being quickly ruined that I realised how the situation was days away from spiralling out of control.

I had been using incoming revenue to not only buy stock, but equipment too. Then learning on the job and delivering orders. The margin for error in my plan to make a rapid sideways assault into the mainstream t-shirt printing business was zero.

In a few months, with a bad plan and terrible execution, the printing enterprise went from being a really nice money making asset with virtually no possibility of personal risk, into a black hole that had me sitting in a Police station cell block for 4 hours trying to pinpoint the exact moment everything started to go wrong.

There is one other point that has always stuck with me from the experience. A key difference between service and product businesses is that when you get it wrong with a service business, you can in most cases rectify the situation by working harder.

On the other hand, the only thing that can fix a broken product is money.

Starting Your Service Empire

Service empires really are very easy to start. It all begins the day you start helping other people to get something that they want, whether that be photographs of their products, more website traffic or better bookkeeping. In most cases, all that's required is a set of skills and the tools to implement them. Some fields will have too much regulation to make it worthwhile, but even so the potential choices are vast. We need to refine this selection with our single fixed requirement. The ability to run the empire from anywhere in the world. This reduces the number of potential business models significantly, but still leaves you with a huge number of options to choose from.

Your choice will be strongly influenced by the skills you have and the character of work you want to do. I knew nothing about web development and Internet marketing before I began, but I knew that my IT skills were good and I was confident that with enough time I could help other businesses meet their online goals. Had I chosen something in the realm of design though, I would have struggled and probably failed. I'm sure the technical skill set could have been acquired over time, but never being blessed with the "designer's eye" or passion for aesthetics, it's unlikely I would ever reach a level of mastery and commitment that would ensure long term success.

Almost all of the service businesses run by the digital nomads are basically freelance operations. Using their skills, they are helping either a single company, or a client base to solve problems.

Most freelancers walk a fine line between being a technician and a consultant and often it's difficult to distinguish between the two. The nomads I have met so far; all fall into the following fields. This is by no means an exhaustive list though, any service that can be fulfilled independently of any one location can be made to work.

- Online Teachers and Tutors

- Online mentors

- Accountants and bookkeepers

- HR consultants

- Career Consultants

- Designers and Illustrators

- Web Developers

- Software developers

- App developers

- Game developer

- Search Engine Optimisers

- Digital Marketers

- Copywriters

- Hypnotherapists

- Translators

- Photographers

- Sales Operatives

- Recruitment Consultants

- Videographers and Film makers

- Audio technicians

All of these freelance service empires have the potential to grow into larger agencies, but that would require the mobilisation of additional employees and opens the door for the complications we discussed above.

The reason many of the nomads haven't scaled their enterprises to the agency level is that it will almost certainly detract from the freedom they have already secured for themselves.

I have recently made the decision to take on additional employees, but it was something I had delayed for many years. Time will tell whether this is a smart decision or not. The model I have created though, mitigates many of the risks that I was woefully ignorant of in my first few unsuccessful imperial campaigns. The tactics being employed include allowing the team to work from home, billing the clients for each hour they work and encouraging the team to communicate directly with them. This removes overhead costs, limits the venture's risk exposure and takes me out of the operational equation.

My margins are locked into the hourly rate, so I never need to pay for a single hour that isn't generating profit. All of the work that is being done, is within a new sub market and while still very related, is separate to my core business. The reason why I never up-sold the service in the past is that I didn't have the time to provide it. Now though, by executing a well thought out plan, I have a new asset that cost me nothing, risks me nothing and will generates passive revenue for years to come. Not only this, but with time the asset will improve, become more efficient and ultimately, more valuable.

You need absolute clarity about what it is your enterprise will be providing the market place. You should be able to fill in the blanks in the following statement without hesitation.

"I will be using my ..... skills to help businesses ....."

So for example:

"I will be using my *graphic design* skills to help businesses create their *company logos*"

If you can do this exercise with ease, then you are on your way to operating with clarity about what it is that you can offer the market place. Unfortunately though, we can't stop there. The world is a big place and your empire is competing in the global marketplace. There are simply too many graphic designers making generic company logos. The battlefield is too large and the existing forces too entrenched. To gain an edge you need to find a niche that's big enough to profit from, while being small enough to dominate.

Let's make the service statement more specific:

"I will be using my ..... skills to help ..... businesses ....."

This time we need to think about the particular type of clients we want to help and therefore the sub market we need to target. So for example:

"I will be using my *graphic design skills* to help *software start-ups* create their *brand identity*".

Targeting all businesses who might need new logos is sailing without a compass. Providing brand identities for software start-ups however, is a recipe for success as long as you have the skills to do the job. Neglecting 99% of the market is a counter intuitive strategy, but it's the only sensible one for new business owners with limited resources.

Any market at its top level is too broad for you to make an impact in without a war chest to cover the mass marketing expenses needed to succeed. It doesn't matter if you're a graphic designer, web developer or recruitment adviser, without a specific niche to focus on you are placing yourself in the global race to the bottom. Nothing distinguishes you from the legion of overseas operatives who can provide the same general service, to the same general clients, at a much lower price. Aligning your business with a particular niche on the other hand automatically places you in the category of "specialist". There may be far fewer people at any one time looking to build a responsive e-commerce website using Magento, but those that are will be much more likely to buy from someone who specialises in responsive e-commerce Magento web development. Not only this, but as the client has hired the services of an "specialist", they will expect to pay higher prices. The client simply can't compare your service prices with those of another web developer, who very well may be able to provide the same service, but had instead elected to market their skills generally.

Assuming you have the skills and tools, your success will depend on your ability to choose a lucrative sub niche and present your business as a credible provider to that market. It's no good being a self-employed "recruitment consultant", you need to be instead, something like a "recruitment consultant that helps UK candidates secure employment with Hong Kong Asset Management firms". Only with this clarity could you make any meaningful tactics to penetrate the market. In the case of the recruitment consultant, she knows exactly which companies in Hong Kong to build relationships with while also being a magnet for all of the prospective asset managers in the UK who have a taste for the orient.

Similarly, an SEO consultant has far more chances of securing a loyal client base if they focus on a particular kind of industry in a particular country, simply for the fact that the given consultant can demonstrate that they have a clear track record helping that particular kind of business, within that particular market.

Offering all things, to all men may seem like a prudent approach in the early stages of your business as you try to hedge your bets and drive early sales. However, this not only lacks imagination, but also waters down the perceived value of your services in the marketplace. When you think about it, all businesses require niche services. No one just wants a website, they want a website for their particular business, in their particular market. Find that market and concentrate your forces.

When I started my marketing company, I fell into the same trap most entrepreneurs do in the early stages of their business. Desperate for sales I created page after page on my website, offering everything and anything from logo design and email marketing to Google AdWords and SEO. It was only when I stripped all of this noise away and focused almost exclusively on Google AdWords and PPC marketing that things started to happen for me. It was easier to rank my website on Google because the whole website was optimised around specific niche keywords. It was easier to close customers, because they wanted professional PPC services and I could demonstrate with little effort that I was a PPC specialist. In most cases I didn't even need to demonstrate this point because 5 seconds spent on my website would tell the client that my whole business was Google AdWords PPC.

By making it look like the only thing I specialised in was PPC consultancy, I cornered the market in every channel my services were advertised.

But this is not the whole story. From the face of it, we were an online advertising agency with a small range of very specialist services. Once the client had purchased from us however and we had established trust, the same client was carefully up-sold a tailored suite of marketing solutions. The strategy was essentially to sell new customers on our expertise in a narrow field and then retain existing customers with solutions to every conceivable marketing related problem they may have. I essentially wanted my agency to be their marketing department. However, if the initial service offering to the new client was, "whatever you want, we can do it", the business just wouldn't have attracted the same quantity or calibre of clients.

Niche positioning, as I have tried to explain is absolutely critical. It's the single most powerful strategic move you can make in the early days of your business. Having said that though, once you have created a brand presence within a given sub niche, there's no reason why you can't position yourself in many different niches and then broadly up-sell to your client later. Care needs to be taken though. A successful Sushi restaurant will lose customers fast if it starts offering pizza on the menu. But no one will bat an eyelid, much less even know, if the same restaurant owner opens a pizza place around the corner.

The key is to differentiate it from your existing enterprise with separate branding. For this you will probably just need a separate website, stationery and email address.

Let's say you have a successful enterprise creating apps for the real estate industry, but have also identified potential in creating apps for chiropractors. Both are similar services from a technical point of view, but from the client's it's a world of difference. In this case you need two distinct brand identities and two different websites'. When either a real estate agent or chiropractor is looking to get their app developed, they are much more likely to choose the company that specialises in providing solutions for that particular industry. They never need to know it's all just smart marketing.

Marketing Your Service Empire

Every day, promoting your business becomes harder as more of your competitors clutter the marketplace with their products, services, brand messages and marketing campaigns. Ranking your pages on search engines now often requires hiring expensive SEO specialists to make your pages even remotely visible for the most profitable keywords (Not your company name. No one will search your company name, except to find your address and send you a bill) in your marketplace.

Despite being an SEO consultant myself, I found it extremely difficult to rank my web pages prominently for the categories of Google AdWords, SEO and Web Design in the city of Sheffield, let alone the world.

It is of course harder to compete against sophisticated Internet marketers than it would be to try and rank a local cleaning company, but the fact is that in almost every industry now you will struggle to rank your site and make your pages visible organically.

This challenge is overcome to quite a large degree, by how well you have positioned your business in a lucrative sub niche. In the case of the brand identity consultant for software start-ups, they are almost certain, with little effort to rank at least somewhere on the first or second page of Google for that specific keyword, say in the USA. It would be almost impossible though, for the same consultant to rank nearly as highly for the simple keyword "brand identity consultant", much less "logo designer".

When you start your service business, you should have a website that presents your operation as credible and competent. It's also an important platform for demonstrating social proof and offering visitors more information about you and your services. However, you should not solely rely on it to generate sales and certainly not bet on organic traffic as your major source of revenue for the first year at least. Instead, your website needs to be part of a network of assets that drives customers from multiple channels of concentrated traffic. Organic search is one such channel, advertising, social media, PR, affiliate marketing and freelancing portals are others that may need to be part of the mix.

Freelancing portals like People Per Hour have been the backbone of my business for a long time and I'm a huge advocate.

The reason is that they allow you to tap into large volumes of traffic that are all, almost by definition looking for solutions to their business problems. There are now a wide range of different platforms, including:

- People per hour

- Freelancer

- Guru

- Elance

- Upwork

- Fiverr

It costs absolutely nothing to promote your services on these websites. You will have to pay a small percentage of commission to the freelancing portal, but this can (or should) be absorbed within your pricing.

Any work you secure from these portals is work you would never have received in any other channel.

If you are running a service business and have not identified relevant 3rd party portals, then you will assuredly be losing out on commercial opportunity over the next few months. Just building your businesses profile on all of the online portals relevant to your services could be the single most valuable investment of your time this year. The results will be relative to the effort put in. The more you polish your profile and add carefully worded sales copy with credibility indicators, you will secure more leads. As you generate good reviews, your sales are likely so increase exponentially. They certainly did in my case, by the time I had 100 five star reviews, I was spending a great deal of my time on one particular freelancing portal.

Like your website, these portals should be regarded as an important piece of a network of marketing assets. You will also need to think about how to promote your services on appropriate social media platforms. Not all will be suitable for your business. Pinterest and Instagram are well suited to creative, design based service providers, whereas LinkedIn is more suited to B2B enterprises. It's much better to concentrate your forces in the platforms where you can gain the most leverage and achieve the highest return for your efforts.

Education marketing is another powerful tool for service providers.

Teaching people how to solve their own problems seems a counterintuitive way to build leads, but actually it establishes you as an expert in the marketplace, broadens your reach and probably provides additional passive revenue too.

YouTube is a natural place for this, though that is not to discount other text based platforms. One of the best marketing plays I made was creating a course on Udemy teaching people how to set up their own Google AdWords campaigns. When I told people about my plan they thought I was crazy, "giving away my secrets". The only thing that was crazy was that kind of myopic thinking.

My client base wasn't on Udemy and they certainly didn't have the time or inclination to do it themselves. Tapping into that platform though opened the door to thousands of new leads, all of which were interested in using Google AdWords for their businesses.

In addition to that, the course makes passive revenue and helps me close more clients as I can demonstrate unequivocally that I am the expert they need.

Concentration of forces is essential to gaining a lasting foothold in the market. This doesn't mean you only have to do one thing; it simply means that in all of your actions; effort should be concentrated only on the key points of leverage. One of your first jobs should be to identify where these impact areas are and then devise a plan that focuses your energy on these points of leverage.

It's likely that the successful model for selling the service you want fulfil has already been mapped out a long time ago. Find the entrepreneurs who are already doing well in your chosen market and model them.

You will probably spot opportunities to make improvements too, building on their work and insights and gaining a strategic edge over them and your less thoughtful competitors.

Product Empires

For anyone who's objective is personal freedom, products trump services almost every time. Once created or acquired, each item in stock equates to a unit of value that simply needs to be shipped to your customer. All of your growth comes from marketing, sales and new product development. By focusing on these higher level tasks, you are generally working "on" the business and not "in" it, which you would most assuredly be doing when you are operating a service enterprise.

I moved my empire into products much later than I would have liked. Consulting has been enjoyable over the last few years, but the hit of excitement felt after securing a new client is always followed by a crash of realism, when you remember you actually have to do some hard work now.

Scaling and automation are problematic too because you are usually dealing with too many variables, people and problems. It was possible to turn the individual services into product-like service packages, with templates, standardized documentation and delivery processes, but in the end, you still have to do the work. Time is split between finding new clients and serving existing ones. The ratio of time of course is dictated by the number of existing customer billable hours you have booked in. Unless you have a sales team, any time left is spent on finding new ones and devising ways to extract more revenue from each client faster.

One aspect of my grand plan was to use the consulting business, and other information assets I had acquired (discussed in the next chapter) to bridge the time needed to extend the empire into products and allow me to stop consulting completely.

Working on that bridge though, became a never ending task as taking action on the other side was always pushed back "a few more months, probably". The cost of living in England didn't help the situation either. In fact, it was only when I made the move to Chiang Mai and cut my cost of living by 60% that there was the spare capital to acquire stock, samples and cover advertising & marketing expenses for a few months without needing the project to turn a meaningful profit straight away. As with all of my commercial experiments, mistakes were made and the model needed a fair amount of refining before I could consider it an efficient asset and focus on the process of scaling.

The first product choices I made were not viable and I've still got piles of unsold stock, that doesn't fit within context of any of my sales channels.

I suspect it will sit there and slowly diminish as people buy them on Ebay over the next 2 years. It takes time and money to put all the pieces into place; Polishing your product range, building attractive digital shop fronts and engaging with a large enough pool of prospective customers, all the while putting food on your table and a roof over your head.

There are many different types of product empires, though not all lend themselves to securing freedom equally. Physically manufacturing products has been the predominant model for creating economic value throughout human history. Using their own (or more likely somebody else's) capital, an entrepreneur mobilises the necessary resources needed to manufacture a given product, bringing it to market, in the pursuit of profits.

This has traditionally required the building or acquiring of a factory and then the tooling and staffing needed to make it operational. A big undertaking to be sure, but the rewards to the entrepreneur who pulled it off in a world of cheap, non-unionised labour were immense. The high barriers to entry though made it almost impossible for normal individuals to ever take part in such a lucrative pastime.

The model was so successful that during the Industrial revolution, the fate of whole towns were linked to the fortunes of the local manufacturing businesses. In my home city of Sheffield, many of the buildings were built using the wealth generated by the capitalist Mark Firth, a man who pioneered the now famous Sheffield steel industry.

Many of the present day high schools (mine included) and hospitals occupy the palatial mansions that made up part of his wealth. Not only this, but as the Sheffield steel industry grew, so too did the need for housing.

To this day many areas of Sheffield still preserves the "Firth" name. Villages and small towns were created around the factories that employed them. Employment was for life. This story has played itself out across the developed world from the cotton mills of Manchester to the car factories of Detroit. Thankfully though the industrial revolution is now over.

When you first start your enterprise, there is almost no reason for you to actually physically produce products in a factory that you own.

As we all know, even the largest companies and brands contract out their manufacturing to Chinese firms. For you, the cash strapped entrepreneur, the start-up costs are often insurmountable. Not only will the initial tooling and capital requirements be prohibitive, but in the early stages of your business, your product is largely untested. Saddling up with that much risk and liability at this stage is foolish. Once you have reached a certain scale of course, there may be many operational and financial benefits to be had from producing 'in house'. But this should happen later, when you either have a good enough sales history to secure a loan or preferably use retained capital from within your business.

As with all the advice in this book of course, there are caveats and counter arguments. Some products do lend themselves to being produced in house.

Items that sell well on platforms like ETSY are often hand made by people at home or small workshops. With the right skills, high end soaps and candles for instance can be made easily with cheap moulds. Jewellery, accessories even furniture or instruments (if that is something you are passionate about) can be produced relatively cheaply with a set of tools, YouTube and lots of practice. These are rare examples though and in almost all other cases, you will need to find a manufacturing partner.

Once you have your product niche fully researched, you should identify a list of contract manufacturers that have the required capabilities to help you. These companies exist simply to manufacture for third parties like yourself and almost all of them specialize within specific product sectors, ranging from golf clubs and calendars to wicker baskets and garlic presses.

Almost every conceivable item can be brought to the market with enough cash and the right manufacturing partner. It will of course be a challenge to find the best supplier and it's likely you will have to test a number of different companies before committing large amounts for your resources with one of them. Paying for samples first is often standard practice and highly advisable. The reasons for this should be obvious. There are also a number of companies that can act as your agent in China and check whether the firms you are dealing with are real and reputable while also ensuring the quality of the products, before they get dispatched from the factory. As you wager more skin in the game, these services can be vital to mitigate risk and insure against the likely calamities that doing business directly with China may well entail. While there are of course many routes to market for your products, retailing online lends itself the most to securing personal freedom.

If the product is right and you are sure of the foot traffic, a high street store could be made to work. But your overheads will be high and for the first year at least, you will probably have to open up every day, collect the cash and manage the staff. Better than working in an office, for sure. But we can do better than that.

One of the most exciting developments to come to e-commerce and a business model of choice among experienced digital nomads is Fulfilment by Amazon (FBA). FBA entrepreneurs manufacture or white label products, usually in China and then ship the entire inventory directly to Amazon's fulfilment warehouses in the UK and USA. When a customer purchases the products on Amazon (and other outlets), the items are shipped directly to the customer from the Amazon warehouse.

A large percentage of the products on the Amazon inventory are FBA products, you may have seen them yourself advertised as "Amazon Prime" and with a note that the product is "fulfilled by Amazon".

The products people are selling are by no means, necessarily new inventions. I know many different people making relatively large amounts of money selling products ranging from glossy hair wax to cotton rattan fairy lights. A successful FBA business model can be executed in the following way:

Identify a niche - Using tools like Jungle Scout and AMZ tracker you can identify product niches that have large numbers of sales, but relatively low (or poor) competition. Not all product niches will be suitable, but never rule out a product because it seems too bland or uninteresting.

If the software tells you there is a huge amount of sale and the few competitors selling that product have bad reviews, you could have found a little gold mine. Act swiftly. You should also record any important keyword categories that you have discovered during the research process. These will be extremely important when it comes to optimising your product listing.

Identify contract manufacturers - This is obviously one of the most important things to get right and has the potential to be the hardest stage in the establishment of your new empire. It is simple and certainly advisable to find a list of manufacturing contacts using the Alibaba portal (the largest wholesale and manufacturing marketplace online), but it has always smelled something of the wild west to me.

There are some excellent companies on there, but extreme care, caution and cynicism should be taken. Despite this though Alibaba is a great first point of call to map out the potential options and get some initial price points. When it comes to actually selecting the manufacturing partner, don't forget to conduct thorough due diligence. It may also be wise to hire the services of a 3rd party quality assurance firm to make sure that what your contacts are telling you is the truth. Another excellent method for finding manufacturers and OEM suppliers are the huge export trade shows, such as Canton Fair in Guangzhou, China. These colossal events feature almost every non consumable product on the retail shelves today and probably the most direct, efficient and safest way to build supplier relations in China.

Run the maths - At this stage you should have a fairly good idea of the kind of product you want to bring to the marketplace, the suppliers who can help you and clarity on how much you will need to pay for different order quantities. The more you buy of course, the cheaper the products will be, but your business should still be viable at the minimum order quantity level. This data will make it possible to start estimating your products potential profitability. A spreadsheet is the tool most suited to this kind of analysis. Remember to bear in mind the import laws of your country, as there may be additional taxes to pay. Using this data, you should be able to work out the answers to the following questions:

- What is the average price of similar products listed by competitors?
- What is my profit margin? (factoring in shipping,

taxes, listing & FBA fees)

- Where is my break-even point? (How many products do I need to sell to get my money back)

- How much will I make if sell the entire inventory?

- At what point should I consider restocking? (Taking into account known lead times)

Design a better product - Once you know which product you are going to bring to the market, you need to make sure it is genuinely better, perhaps solving a new problem or improving the aesthetics. Offering long term value is essential to smooth, sustainable operations and bad reviews will kill your business. Almost all of the information you need to make a product that solves the problems of existing items will be within the reviews for those products.

If you are going to produce a new laptop case for the latest MacBook for instance, reading at least 300 (preferably 1000) of the related Amazon product reviews will tell you all that you need know about features people like and how the design can be improved. In many cases you may just need to add your logo to an existing product and perhaps design better packaging. If you have Photoshop skills or the time and willingness to learn, you can do this yourself. In some cases, you might need to hire the services of a professional on one of the freelancing portals we discussed earlier, such as people per hour. Attractive packaging and branding can make all the difference when it comes to customers making the decision between you and a competitor.

Order samples - You're almost certainly going to have to pay for samples and will probably have to order quite a few before you are finally ready to purchase the first 5,000 units. They can be expensive (between $50 and $150 per sample), but to try and make any savings on this point is not only a false economy, but also super risky. If all of your limited capital just went into selecting the best product and manufacturing it perfectly the first time, the money would have been invested wisely. Hard work can take care of the marketing for the first few months.

Order your products - An empire is being born. At this point you're ready to request an invoice outlining crystal clear manufacturing costs. As long as you have done your due diligence properly, you are happy with the sample and your instincts says "yes", there's nothing holding you back from placing you first order.

Polishing your product - Whichever contract manufacturer you have used, it is likely that they are experts in producing only that type of product. They will probably not be the best company to make your product packaging for you. How you brand and polish your products will impact how attractively it is perceived by the market and essentially how well it sells. Repeat these steps, using the specifications of your product to design and manufacturer packaging that puts the gold seal on them. Stickers, hang tags and other freebies included within the packaging raise the perceived quality of your product and are usually extremely inexpensive.

List your products on Amazon - As soon as your stock arrives and you have assembled all of the different aspects of your product (packaging, inserts, tags, marketing materials) you are ready to start adding products to Amazon.

The first step will be to take great product shots. This can be done at home if you have a decent camera (most modern smart phones will do the job with a lightbox or similar contraption) or you can hire a professional. On Amazon you must use images that have a crisp white background. All of my product shots were done at home using a cheap lightbox and then edited later on Adobe Photoshop, essentially cutting the product out and then remounting it on a white background. Armed with your images and the research from stage 1, you are ready to register for an account with Amazon Seller Central and start listing your products. Don't rush the creation of your listing, make sure you optimise the keywords and write great sales copy. Research how the top sellers in your category have developed their listing and emulate them.

Dispatch to Amazon - Once you are setup with Amazon Seller Central, you can apply to upgrade your account to be FBA eligible. With this confirmed you can dispatch your whole (or part) of you inventory to the Amazon fulfilment centres in the USA and UK. There are extremely strict guidelines for how you do this however, care must be taken that your products are packaged and labelled properly. Failing to do this could mean your products are returned, causing disappointment, delays and probably additional expenses. When your products have been received and approved you will be notified by email. Congratulations, you are officially an FBA entrepreneur with a promising mini empire. But we're not finished yet.

Link Amazon FBA to other platforms - You can link other ecommerce platforms to the Amazon FBA system. The most popular of these are linking ETSY, Ebay and Shopify accounts but it also possible to link your own website to the Amazon checkout. This means that when you make sales through these other platforms, Amazon will still ship the product directly to the client for you. It is for this reason that FBA has become the business model of choice among entrepreneurs who are seeking personal freedom.

Identify Other Sales Channels - FBA gives you the power to sell online without needing to think about logistical restraints. It also allows you to tap into the millions of people searching products on Amazon and other networks every day. But this is not enough.

As we discussed in the chapter on Service Empires, you should position your product in every relevant market place that has concentrated volumes of qualified traffic. #ETSY is a natural choice for many people, while Ebay would be more suitable for others. You have already taken your product shots, identified your keywords and written great sales copy, so reuse that hard work and get your product on as many marketplaces as you can, as long as there is genuine relevance between what you are selling and what people are looking for. For some platforms integrating with Amazon will be relatively straightforward. In other cases though, you may have to use a 3rd party software such as 'ShipStation'. There are also countless other networks, while not necessarily 'ecommerce' platforms, will be a source of good quality leads. These networks could include Facebook, Twitter, Reddit or even YouTube. You need to identify a list of carefully chosen channels that offer the highest leverage for your type of product and then concentrate your effort on them.

Develop your own e-commerce platform - If you have followed the advice in these steps and you have implemented a smart marketing strategy your business should be viable on Amazon (and a few other marketplaces) alone. It is still highly advisable though that you feature your products on your own e-commerce website too. Not only will you have more control over the content and pricing, but this should allow to tap into additional organic traffic while offering a platform to build your brand. This mitigates one of the key problems of just selling on Amazon, that while it is easy to push sales, it is difficult to build a brand. WordPress websites enhanced with the free Woocommerce plugin are very common among FBA-ers, Shopify is also a popular choice for those of you who have limited web development skills.

Grow your product range - By now your product is on sale, available to the world. Your marketing strategy has been devised and you have started to generate capital. There's only one thing left for you to do; create more products.

This is but one model though. As with physically manufacturing, acquiring products from someone else and reselling them is older than money itself. Buying products for resale will never secure you the same amount of operating profit that a manufacturer can achieve, but there are many benefits that may make this the right model for you.

As a retailer you can select products which are already proven in the market place, making it easy for you to research who the existing players are, which distribution channels are successful and how to price your merchandise, because people are already selling and others are buying.

As a retailer you will be also able to secure your initial inventory in smaller quantities, thus limiting your risk exposure. For the FBA manufacturer on the other hand the minimum order quantities will often be much higher.

I wasn't ready to start manufacturing because I wanted to save the majority of the capital I had to ensure that I had enough cash to spare if the tendrils of misfortune found a way to reach me here in Asia.

A few hundred dollars spent purchasing a small amount of inventory though, wouldn't make much difference and allowed me to put skin into the game of e-commerce. I have since built relationships with many local vendors and manufacturers and tested a number of different product ideas.

The first purchase was on a whim. I found a seller who made canvas backpacks and negotiated an excellent wholesale price with her. With such a low price, how could I lose? Well I did lose. Months later 99% of the bags are still in my apartment taking up space and reminding me to stop buying things without looking at the big picture. I have largely abandoned the bags and few others now because they don't fit in with the portfolio of carefully selected items that I have since been curating.

It would be unfair to say the money was wasted though. Guided by this experience, my product choices since then have been much better, more thought-out and thankfully selling well. The lesson learned was that it is all well and good "getting a good deal", but you need to think what you are going to do when you actually have them and ready to sell.

When it comes down to it the questions remain, "is this really something I want to sell?" and almost as importantly, "do I have any leverage selling them?". The answer to both, was "no". I had (and have) zero motivation to spend time promoting those bags and certainly don't want to add them to the current range which took me so long to get right.

I tried other products in the first few months that did sell well, but I abandoned them due to a number of issues. These included the availability of acquiring additional stock at short notice and the prohibitively high cost of postage which really ate into my margins. All of which though were valuable lessons and made it possible for me to outline a framework of requirements which guided later procurement decisions forming a profitable product range.

- The first principle was that the products needed to be

made in Chiang Mai, because the level of craftsmanship here is exceptional and I wanted to support the local economy rather than send money to china.

- They needed to be small enough to post in an envelope rather than a box. This reduces the cost of shipping dramatically and allows me to profit on the postage too.

- I wanted consistency between the different product ranges so they could all feature on the same e-commerce platforms and contribute to building a common brand.

- One size fits all. After experimenting with selling shirts and footwear, I realised that the necessity of stocking different sizes wasn't ideal and the chances of returned items was much higher.

- High margins. While this seems like an obvious point,

it's important to note that often the cost of bringing the product to the market will exceed the cost of the product in the first place. My target is around the level of a 600% to 800% mark-up (preferably higher). Many of my products cost $2 and retail for $29 which leaves plenty of room for covering advertising and distribution expenses

My products are listed in Amazon and two ETSY shops, complimented by a WordPress e-commerce website. I purchased the second ETSY store from a digital nomad who had run out of money and was leaving town in a hurry. It has since proven to be one of the best investments I have made to date, returning all of my capital in the first month and growing steadily.

The work he had done developing the store, curating reviews and polishing the products with excellent artwork, care cards, hang tags and packaging could all be absorbed into the empire raising the general levels of quality and value and provide an excellent secondary platform to sell my existing inventory. The revenue is not enough to live on alone, a fact that necessitated the quick sale I'm sure, but it is an elegant addition to a portfolio of assets already generating revenue relatively passively.

In addition to simply buying stock at wholesale prices and then reselling them there are a number of other avenues that may be suitable for you. White labelling for instance is the middle ground between reselling and manufacturing products. Essentially adding your own label to existing items and then resell them under your own brand.

Margins will often be slimmer than they would be if you contracted a manufacturer to produce your inventory from scratch, but minimum order quantities will be lower and there is arguably less risk and room for error. Another feasible option, though harder to secure would be a license agreement with a manufacturer giving you the sole rights to sell a particular product in a given state, country or region. Finding the product that isn't available already in your chosen market and striking a deal will be a challenge, but if you can find the right manufacturer, perhaps a new start up looking for help to distribute in unfamiliar geographic market could be tempted to make a deal with huge long term profits protected from competitors. It is also possible the other way too, taking your own product or invention to a company who license it and pay you a dividend for each unit sold.

Like FBA which we discussed above, drop shipping is a popular business model with people who work for themselves and dislocate time from the acquisition of money. Drop shipping involves 3 parties; The manufacturer, the vendor and the customer. As a "drop shipper" You are the vendor, selling the manufacturers products across your distribution network, whether this is your website, social media platforms or any of the e-commerce sites likes Ebay, Amazon and Etsy. When customers purchase product from your business, an order is sent to the manufacturer who ships directly to the customer. As long as there is an acceptable profit margin and your distribution channels receive enough qualified traffic, you can have a successful business.

Drop shipping is an elegant business model that is attractive to entrepreneurs in the early stages of their journey.

You are selling products on a marginal (one at a time) basis, so discounting the time taken to develop your website and build supplier relationships, there is very little risk. If you have the skills to build and market your own website, then it should be a "no money down" venture. This creates its own problems though. The downsides of a "no money down" business model of course, is the relative ease with which others can enter the market. There is almost no barrier to entry, so the result is legions of drop shippers selling products in almost every market, from light bulbs to drones. Drop shipping has been a buzzword in the online enterprise world for over a decade and in my opinion, the opportunities are drying up as the market becomes saturated with too many people selling the same products. Having said that though, drop shipping is an excellent way to dip your toe into a market and experiment with new product ranges. The co-working spaces in Chiang Mai are filled with western entrepreneurs incubating their drop shipping businesses by taking advantage of the significantly lower cost of living. With the right niche, smart marketing and a lot of hard work, this model can be made to work.

Information Empires

For the entrepreneur who wants to grow and scale their businesses, while not working proportionately more, products are much more suitable models for your new empire than services. There is another option though that lends itself even more to acquiring personal freedom - Information. There is an insatiable demand for knowledge. Every year that passes, we want more of it, faster. The Internet (digital communication) represents our 4th information revolution after printing, writing and speech. Each of these revolutions broadened societies ability to retain and dispense knowledge. Today, we enjoy unprecedented access to information on demand and there is almost no skill that cannot be acquired through some form of online education, usually for free and at the touch of a few buttons.

Successful information products sell for a lot, the marginal cost (cost to sell 'one more' of them) is zero and they are extremely easy to distribute, making them both efficient and lucrative assets to own. The problem comes back to value and strategy though, as it is certainly not easy to sell enough information products to live comfortably for the rest of your life. Like any enterprise, the success of your information empire will depend on how much value it brings to the market place. The knowledge and skills that your information products provide, gives value to the customer by enabling them to do something they previously couldn't do.

My first foray into the information sector was a website that aimed to document and 'digest' the UK's climate laws and regulation. I was working in compliance (corporate regulation) at the time for an Insurance company and recognised that it was a growing sector.

Unfortunately, though quite deservedly, the website never came close to taking off. Not only did I have zero interest in climate change legislation, but the regulatory landscape was simply too vast for me to document on my own. Even if I had recorded and analysed all of it, I would never have been able to keep the website up to date, while maintaining my day job. The problems went deeper though. Not only had I bitten off far more than I could chew in terms of the complex (and boring) nature of the industry, but at the time I had no idea how to market the website, much less profit from it. SEO, sales funnels, ad revenue and conversion optimisation were all still alien concepts to me.

I still think the website is a good idea and could easily have evolved into a profitable eco-system that incorporated recruitment services, training and industry events.

What was missing was the skill and passion needed to drive it forward. I certainly lacked the skill and my passion didn't extend any further than it being the current promising project I was working on at that time. The idea was sound and the skills could, with time have been acquired, but ultimately I just didn't have much interest in climate laws and legislation. When my web development and marketing consultancy started to become busier, there was little time for anything else and the project was forgotten about, leaving the domain and hosting to quietly expire. I knew that making money from information was far smarter than making money from selling my time and labour. Despite this though, it was years before I started to make it a priority.

In 2014 I was browsing Reddit and noticed a post from a man offering 75% off his Google AdWords training course.

By this time, I had streamlined my consultancy, dropping almost all web development and SEO services in favour of becoming a specialist online advertising agency. Google AdWords was a crucial part of my service offering so my curiosity was peaked. I discovered that the man's course on Udemy cost $197 and he had 20,000 customers. Within seconds I had the calculator loaded on my phone and was running the maths. Even taking into account the fact that I found the course using a discount coupon and many others would have done so too, this guy was making some serious money. Not only this but he had two of them, the other was equally as popular and taught people how to master Google Analytics. I was impressed. More than that though, I was motivated. I knew AdWords inside out and was in the perfect position to create a competing course. I had all of the knowledge and this time, the skills. For the next 3 or 4 weeks I barely left my room as I worked day and night to get my course out as quickly as possible. I knew I had missed the boat to become the leading AdWords product on Udemy, but the door to second place was wide open and I was going to secure it.

My course is still on Udemy and has around 5,000 students. It never tipped the original one off its perch and newcomers have joined the market, but it is an asset that has generated passive income every month since being published and it will continue to do so for many years to come.

In addition to the new cash flow, the course has served me well in my other businesses. It provides a large source qualified leads to sell services to and makes it much easier to close consultancy clients, by significantly increasing perceived credibility. I did after all, write the course.

Udemy is the world largest online course platform with around 6 million active students taking all manner of digital lessons. The platform makes it extremely easy for individuals to make money teaching the subjects they have expertise in. I've created a number of other course and plan to make more. This book may very well find itself being the basis for the next one.

Duplicating the content across similar online course marketplaces such as Skillshare and Skillfeed was also a success. Never quite making as much money as Udemy, but adding more passive revenue to the growing stream of income. Unfortunately Skillfeed has closed down now, but the list of potential platforms is vast, perhaps becoming even more exciting with Amazon making a move into the digital education arena.

The second piece of my information empire started almost as spontaneously as the AdWords course. My gym partner called me up to show me a website he him and his friends had started using. It was a was a premium membership site teaching Matched Betting, a system that made it possible to cash in the free promotional bets offered by online bookmakers like William Hill and Ladbrokes. The system basically worked by placing bets with the introductions promotional vouchers, then going to a betting exchange like Betfair and placing a hedge bet. You could essentially convert around 70 percent of the vouchers face value to cash. As long as you get the maths right, you were guaranteed to make money whatever the outcome of the event. I signed up for the free account on the website and very sceptically, tested out the system. To my surprise and delight, it worked. The business was essentially a membership website with a list of instructions on how to use some online tools to extract the value from each of the hundred or so deals available online at that time.

The competition was charging £16.95 a month for access to all of the matched betting deals and after a bit of research (looking at the number of people in their premium members Facebook group), I learned they had thousands of members. They were making a lot. I knew I could build a better membership site and had all of the marketing skills needed to make it a success. Locking myself in my room again, I got to work and a month later the business was up and running. The usability of the site was improved significantly and I was charging half of the membership fee. It didn't take long for premium members to start signing up. Another asset in the bag developing mostly passive income.

I'm not shy about implementing an almost identical business model. The way I looked at it was that they were making too much money, in an uncontested market, with a product that I had all of the skills and resources to replicate and improve in less than 30 days. It was the same logic behind the Udemy course and I felt compelled to (and did) act extremely quickly. My attitude to this should be a clear lesson on the disposition of your competitors. Being seen either suffering a weakness or enjoying easy profits will eventually result in someone making a decisive move, perhaps permanently placing themselves in your small niche with more capital and manpower to compete with you. Protecting your 'great idea' is an almost impossible undertaking over the long run in the global marketplace. There are two ways to deal with it. Either building a strategy that focuses on acquiring market share and locks you into a bitter struggle to "one up" each other over the long rub. Or alternatively, make the whole business a small, but profitable and efficient asset within a portfolio of other assets. The former will includes, branding, sales & marketing and skilled employees. It will give you the very best chance of making your business the most successful in the industry. I chose the latter however, because it is a better route to freedom. I'm in the business of acquiring assets and not interested in dedicating my life to running a membership website. The objective was to move in on the opportunity and establish a base that can look after itself and start to generate passive income efficiently. Once the asset was built I never intended to spend more than an hour or two a month on the project, so it was never going to do serious damage to a well-resourced and motivated competitor.

There is a market for almost all types of education, though some niches attract much more interest and have become extremely saturated.

Many information products that help people to make money online or date more women for example are wildly profitable, but for every successful launch, there are thousands of similar products that never take off. Reasons for this include the fact that the successful authors often have huge mailing lists, partnerships with other authors and distribution networks. It is also true though that much of the content published is of low quality, written simply to make money without consideration to providing value for an actual, real human being. In the world of information empires, charlatanism abounds. There is opportunity here though to create a gem in the muck with something that teaches a genuine skill and solves real problems. I would strongly advise avoiding topics such as "make money fast", "dating advice" and "forex" niches which are promoted so unimaginatively through pop-up ads on porn sites and dubious affiliate networks. The reason why the chapter on information empires comes after services and products is because, to develop successfully, is the hardest of all three. This is because generally you need to acquire a completed body of knowledge and skill first. As we talked about earlier, with most products and services, you can learn as you go.

As with products and services, information empires vary greatly. In general, though they fall into two categories, Education and Entertainment. As the distribution of both of these becomes more decentralised and on-demand there are growing opportunities to place a base or two in a couple of niches. Your information can take any form of digital medium such as blogs, e-books, YouTube or pod-casts. Forming a network of appropriate platforms would be ideal allowing you to tap into different channels of traffic and potential users.

If you are creating an education product, the real key is creating content that solves certain peoples' problems. If you are creating an entertainment product, it just needs to be entertaining to a particular audience.

When it comes to marketing your digital product or service it's unlikely you will be able to rely on the traffic generated from the platforms they are featured on. You will need to identify secondary platforms like Reddit, Twitter and Facebook to drive additional visitors to engage with what you have to say. In most cases, such as YouTube, this will not only grow your audience but also prioritise your content in the algorithm of wherever your content is primarily hosted. Be smart about your marketing. Interweave your information assets and use them to funnel sales into other products.

You should also offer diluted content for free to maximise the number of leads at the top of your funnel and carefully plan how you are going to turn these interested individuals, into paying customers.

Once your first course is developed it will be easier to create more, reusing templates, software and newly acquired skills. Each one will make money for you, essentially forever and should grow organically with time. The content can (and should) be duplicated, added to the huge network of online platforms and marketplaces. In addition to this though, there are many different ways to monetise your information products, from web site sales and ad revenue to affiliate income and sponsorship.

The type of product you have and the objective you are trying to reach will largely determine which are the best revenue models for your particular information products. Your strategy should focus energy on the points of leverage that help you to maximise the returns from revenue model you have chosen.

Building a successful information empire will require more patience than developing an enterprise in products and services. In addition to securing traffic, you will also need to establish an audience, that wants to hear what you have to say. You might be able to do it in 6 months, if you act with great skill and dedicate your time to it. It's more likely that it will take a year though, before you really start to see growth. The more you can do to market your products and build you fan base, the quicker you can live off the revenue.

Every journey starts with a first step and until it's taken, nothing will happen. You just need to start making some content, then take it from there. Observe, refine your strategy and adapt. All the while, creating more content.

Launch Anxiety

"Once begun, half done"

Right at this very moment, you could do much worse than putting this book down and start working on your empire. You have a clear framework to begin taking meaningful action towards your goals. Your objectives will tell you where you need to sink your foundations and the strategy will guide the choice of tools needed to raise it from the ground.

The first place to direct your energy is answering the question, "what do you want?" - If you have no place to go, you're screwed, whatever the context. Focus all spare energy on discovering your true objectives, the things you really want in and around your life. This is perhaps the hardest part.

There are after all so many roads you could choose.

Hesitating at the junction is no way to live though, so make a decision. Lock yourself away physically (if you can) or mentally (if you can't) and don't stop obsessing until you have figured it out.

How can you get it? - You now know where you need to go, so all that stands between you and it, is the map and the resources to navigate it. A large part of the geography is out of your hands anyway. Time should be spent identifying where you are hemmed in. The nature of your objective, your capital position and level of skills will all impact which tactics could sensibly be included in your strategy. If you have no cash for instance, your strategy won't, or shouldn't, include mass marketing tactics.

Focus on it every day - It sounds so simple, I know. And it's no big secret either. We all know this is the only way to achieve success, but many of us (like I used to), pretend otherwise, looking for faster paths to the vast array of dreams we like to take out and half-heartedly exercise. The weekly buzz felt imagining "what if my lottery ticket was the one", is characteristic of this. All of it holds us back, delays action and will eventually snuff out your imperial spirit entirely. At a dinner party I was asked if I played. I replied, perhaps overly smugly, that I did not, and thought the lottery was the only tax you volunteered for. I did feel the compulsion though, to draw a line in the sand between myself and the insanely bad investment that is the lottery. The man replied that as he had a ticket that week, he "was much more likely to be rich than someone without one". What the man failed to understand of course, was that going home after the party and working on his empire would have incalculably greater chances of eventually building a fortune.

That kind of thinking, always strikes home the stark difference in mentalities between the employed and self-employed. Misunderstanding the differences between luck and fortune, seeking to be picked by individuals or kissed by fate, all the while watching television and hating on work. Reality is malleable, like an epic Lego construction. You can change it, remove what you don't like and bring the aspects that you do, closer to you. But it takes energy to remove pieces and reconstruct them in a location and manner that suits you. If you don't have the objective, you are building without architect's drawings. If you don't have the construction materials or the skills to utilise them, you are without tactics and strategy respectively.

With no plan you can move the pieces until you're red in the face but you will just be left with a mess at the end of the day that needs cleaning up, or worse, putting back as you found it.

Freedom may not be an easy acquisition, but with a plan, the way is simple. If you pick a business model today and run with it every day, you will almost certainly be in possession of a great little money making asset by the end of the year. Only this will take you one significant step closer to real freedom and ultimately a better life, with you in the driving seat. Most people fall off at this point, never putting skin in the game and getting started. What you start to build in the beginning though, may not be what you end up with later, and in fact this process is normal.

The rise of almost every entrepreneur I know or have read about, is characterised with these features; starting something, faltering once or twice and tweaking the model until success is achieved. They eventually found a way to make it work because they were never, ever going to give up. Pick a good opportunity, work on it competently and commit to it until it can look after itself. There's room to supercharge this process, but ultimately it comes down to that - A clear plan and hard work.

If you are employed and need to spend your most productive hours working for someone else, then you are almost certainly going to have to spend most of your evenings and weekends empire building. It is going to really annoy your friends and loved ones who will invariably see you less for a while. TV is basically out of the question for 6 months at least and even then, it's a habit you should kick over the long run.

In the context of your life's ambitious purpose, spending an evening watching TV is worse than turning on the heating full blast and opening all of the windows in your house. There is always more gas and electricity, but time wasted, is lost forever. Reuse the time saved instead, by pushing the levers on your tactics and firing on the obstacles between where you are, and where you want to be. When you need a break, read a business or marketing book.

This is the essence of the book's lesson. Getting what you want isn't rocket science, you just need to focus effort on something for long enough until you get it. With that bearing fruit you can work on the next one. Prepare yourself for extreme work, allocate enough time and get started on your ingenious scheme, reshaping reality into something more desirable for you and your family.

Links & Resources

This last section compiles some links and resources that might be of use to you, on your pursuit of freedom.

Follow the adventure

When I set off for my new life in Thailand I started making videos and documenting the process. These videos have become a moderately popular YouTube series - Digital Nomad X. While the channel was always part of my strategic plan to expand the information empire, it became much more important to me for other reasons. The videos, particularly in the first few months, became my diary. I used them to relieve any anxiety I felt, essentially being alone in an unfamiliar place. I found it immensely helpful to talk about my experiences and express my thoughts out loud. I've tried to be as honest as possible in the videos, recording the good and the bad with equal objectivity.

For those of you looking to build or relocate your empire to Thailand, there may be some value, and most assuredly some laughs at my expense. I seem to embarrass myself at least once a day, while adjusting to the new culture.

Digital Nomad X YouTube Channel:

http://www.youtube.com/c/digitalnomadxtv

Digital Nomad X Blog:

http://www.digital-nomad-x.com/

Books

You have finished this book, so it's safe to assume we are alike, kindred spirits looking for ways to grow, on a journey to become more than we were before. I was never lucky enough to find a mentor, perhaps one day I will. Until then though, I have relied on books to develop myself into the man I wanted to become.

The books I have listed below are the tip of my literary recommendation iceberg. I have selected them because they were the ones that impacted me the most. I started reading business and personal development books while I was a working in London. It killed time on the daily 3-hour commute and gave me hope, that one day I wouldn't have to get up at 5:45 every day and walk through London's cold, dark streets to a train that would take me an even more undesirable location - the office.

My journey to financial independence started the day I picked up the first 2 books listed below in 2009. I read them over and over again. The 4 Hour Workweek by Tim Ferriss, opened my eyes to an alternative way to live my life. It inspired me to take action and gave me the confidence to resign. How to Get Rich by Felix Dennis on the other hand, prepared me for what was to come. Years of hard work and potential failure after failure, until finally, the skills to make money independently were acquired.

Books which motivated me to take action

Tim Ferriss: 4 Hour Work Week

http://www.amazon.com/4-Hour-Workweek-Escape-Live-Anywhere/dp/0307465357/

Felix Dennis: How to Get Rich

http://www.amazon.com/How-Get-Rich-Greatest-Entrepreneurs/dp/1591842719/

Jason Fried, David Heinemeier Hansson: Rework

https://www.amazon.co.uk/ReWork-Change-Way-Work-Forever-ebook/dp/B003ELY7PG/

Books which gave me the most personal growth

Dale Carnegie: How to Win Friends and Influence People http://www.amazon.com/How-Win-Friends-Influence-People/dp/0671027034/

Napoleon Hill: Think and Grow Rich

http://www.amazon.com/Think-Grow-Rich-Napoleon-Hill/dp/1532876556/

Stephen R. Covey: Habits of Highly Successful People

https://www.amazon.co.uk/Habits-Highly-Effective-People-Interactive-ebook/dp/B01069X4H0/

Lessons in Strategy

Alastair Campbell: Winners

https://www.amazon.co.uk/Winners-They-Succeed-Alastair-Campbell-ebook/dp/B00OWNQZHI/

Richard P Rumelt: Good Strategy / Bad Strategy

https://www.amazon.co.uk/Good-Strategy-Bad-Difference-Matters/dp/B0073V9DQQ/

Money Management

George Samuel Clason: Richest Man in Babylon

https://www.amazon.co.uk/Richest-Man-Babylon-Bestselling-Financial/dp/1615890424/

About The Author

David Black is a location independent entrepreneur (digital nomad) living in Thailand. He is the producer of the popular YouTube Channel "Digital Nomad X" and in his first book, the *21st Century Emperor*, he shares the inspiring story of how he left the corporate world in London and started on the path to securing genuine financial and location independence.

Digital Nomad X YouTube Channel:

http://www.youtube.com/c/digitalnomadxtv

Digital Nomad X Blog:

http://www.digital-nomad-x.com/

Printed in Great Britain
by Amazon